MAKE ME WILLING TO BE WILLING

CATHERINE ANNE JINADU

COVENANT PUBLISHING

MAKE ME WILLING TO BE WILLING
Catherine Anne Jinadu

Unless otherwise stated, all scripture quotations are taken from the Holy Bible, New King James Version (NKJV).

ISBN 978-1-907734-35-9
First Edition, First Printing May 2018

Covenant Publishing
samadewunmi@btinternet.com

Cover Design by Covenant Publishing Team
Published by Covenant Publishing
Printed in the United Kingdom

TABLE OF CONTENTS

DEDICATION

Thanking God for the lives of my parents, Leslie James Herrell and Anne Robertson Herrell (nee Grant)

ACKNOWLEDGEMENTS

Grateful thanks to my two editing friends, Dot Mitchell and Gbenga Badejo. Bless you for all the hard work and revisions.

Thank you to Bible College friends, Bryan and Maureen Sheldon and Sandra Mason for your memories of our college days and for driving through the night to attend our wedding.

Thanks too for my publishers Rev Sam Adewunmi UK, and my beloved brother Akin Feyisetan, Ibadan, Nigeria.

Grateful thanks to Dr Stephen Griffiths, General Director of Overseas Missionary Fellowship, for his book 'The Axe and the Tree' which gave me the information on the aftermath of the Rhodesian massacre.

And...

A big "Thank You" to my husband Paul and to all my Nigerian brothers and sisters, sons and daughters. You have enriched my life and taught me so much.

PREFACE

"He who would glorify his God must set his account on meeting many trials. No man can be illustrious before the Lord unless his conflicts be many. If then, yours be a much-tried path, rejoice in it, because you will the better show forth the all-sufficient grace of God. As for His failing you, never dream of it; hate the thought. The God who has been sufficient until now, should be trusted to the end."

Charles Haddon Spurgeon.

On your journey with the Almighty, has He ever asked you to do or give Him something that seemed outrageous, unfair, impossible, just too much?

When we claim that we belong to God, He can probe our commitment. He is GOD and can put us to the test.

I've been there in that very, very uncomfortable place. I would love to share these experiences with you. But first a little background…

Part 1

AM I WILLING TO SURRENDER MY WHOLE LIFE TO YOU?

Chapter 1

THE EARLY YEARS

***"For You formed my inward parts, You covered me in my mother's womb. I will praise You for I am fearfully and wonderfully made. In Your book were written all the days fashioned (determined) for me"* (Psalm 139:13-14, 17).**

My high-sided cot was in my parent's room close to their bed. One of the sides was faulty and I had discovered that I could grasp the bars, haul myself up and push the side as hard as I could; down it would come. I had learned to somersault myself onto their mattress and make my escape.

I must have been three years old. I had awoken and light was streaming in through the half-drawn curtains. It must be morning, but where were they? I clambered across the bed, down the stairs and searched through all the rooms. No one. The kitchen door was wide open, so down the steps and into the garden. There at the very end were the objects of my desire. Purposefully, I tottered down the path, nightgown flapping in the summer sun. I felt deliciously naughty. My parents were chatting over the fence to our neighbours. Suddenly my father turned and spotted me. He came running to meet me with arms outstretched. I remember the delight in his voice as he caught me up, threw me in the air and twirled me round and round. "What are YOU doing here?" It was not in fact morning but late evening, high summer, the sun still hot.

This is my earliest memory – a delighted father; a loving mother.

I have the privilege to be a much wanted and loved child. For the first five years of my life I was the only child; all their love was lavished on me. Every night my mother, and occasionally, my father would sing me to sleep. My mother had only two melodies in her repertoire; hymns and lullabies. I believe it was the hymns that gave me a deep love for God and from a very early age, a desire to know Him. The first time I saw a butterfly I was entranced. I watched this delicate, gossamer creature fly gracefully from blossom to blossom. I tried to catch it but it eluded me. I knew instinctively that God had made it. But where was He? How could I find Him?

My parents were honourable people. My mother was the kindest person I have ever met. My father was a sportsman being captain of The York Rugby Club and captain of the rowing team. So, his Sundays consisted of sport. By the time I was seven, my father was posted to India with the Royal Air Force and my mother was fully occupied with my two young sisters. I was left largely to my own devices. It was then that I joined the Brownies and I had my first introduction into the mysterious world of the Anglican Church. How I loved it! How proud I was that alone, unaided I could navigate The Book of Common Prayer, and Hymns Ancient and Modern; but how to connect with God? He was "up there" somewhere; aloof, scary, and full of mystery.

One dark evening I decided to visit the vicar and ask him my questions. The driveway to the vicarage was long. On either side, trees swayed menacingly. I pressed on and pulled the jangling bell next to the iron barred door. No answer. I tried again - and again. Eventually the housekeeper appeared. "Please," I said, "I want to see the vicar." "Well," she said, "Ee's not in," with that, the door slammed shut.

But light was dawning. By the time I was eight, not only was I taking myself off to church but I had also discovered a chapel where I sometimes went with the boy across the road. There was no mystery here. It was altogether jollier, more friendly - a good social occasion. And then - Sunday School! This was held every Sunday afternoon in the church hall. Well over a hundred children would pile in to listen to spellbinding Bible stories related by Mary Oglesby.

At seventeen, with glossy hair and limpid brown eyes, Miss Oglesby was quite the most beautiful person I had ever seen. I became her most enthusiastic pupil. My hand would shoot up to answer every question and soon I was rewarded with invitations to tea at her parents' home. Walking there in my best dress I felt like a little princess. And indeed, I was treated like one. Her father and mother buzzed around me plying me with home-made scones and delicious cakes

When I was eleven years old I took and passed the scholarship to grammar school. There I made a new friend. Her name was Mary. Walking home from school one day, she gave me the key to heaven.

"I am a Christian," she told me. "I gave my heart to Jesus when I was eight."

She had my attention.

"If God is so loving and kind why did He allow His only Son to die on a cross?"

Mary looked at me.

"The reason Jesus died on the cross was for our sins. We are all sinners. God had to let Jesus die in our place."

Like a light illuminating a room, I too was flooded with light. I knew I was hearing a profound truth. Everything fell into place. So, Jesus was the connection to God!

"How did you 'give your heart to Jesus'?" I wanted to know.

"It's easy. You just say 'Dear Jesus, please forgive my sins. I open my heart to You. Come and live inside me.'"

That Friday I accompanied Mary to The Young People's Mission in Saviourgate, York and committed my life to Christ.

For an eleven year old girl in post war Britain, The

Young People's Mission was a great place to be. Not only were there film shows, and table tennis, sports and free ice cream, but almost every week we had visiting speakers, many of them missionaries. I was surprised to discover that the owner of this vast Victorian house, where we could roam freely was none other than Stanley V. Oglesby, the father of my much-loved Sunday school teacher. One of his great friends was Norman Grubb, the biographer of Rees Howells and son in law of C. T. Studd, the wealthy Cambridge graduate and England cricketer who gave away his fortune and together with six other Cambridge graduates (the famous Cambridge seven) joined Hudson Taylor for missionary work in China. He also served in India and eventually in the Congo where he founded the World Wide Evangelisation Crusade. We learned too about Hudson Taylor who founded the China Inland Mission, William Carey of India and the five young American missionaries who were martyred by the South American tribespeople they were trying to reach for Christ.

When I was fourteen years old, one of our speakers was a diminutive elderly lady who had been a missionary in China. Small she may have been but her zeal was enormous. She blazed with fire. Her name was Gladys Aylward. Previously an uneducated parlour maid, she had a passion to go to China. No missionary society would accept her. Undeterred, she saved up for the fare and travelled out alone. She lived a life of great sacrifice and led hundreds of children to safety to escape the communists. She is the heroine of the film "The Small Woman."

She gave us a challenge:

"God does not want your bits and pieces. God wants all of you."

That phrase was a shock to my system. So, there was more to Christianity than receiving. We had to give something back and I was slowly realising that the 'something' was all of me; my life, my will, my dreams and aspirations. One of the hymns we sang at that time was by George Matheson.

Make me your captive Lord, and then I shall be free
Force me to render up my sword, and I shall conqueror be
My will is not my own, till Thou hast made it Thine
If I would reach a monarch's throne I must my crown resign.

Resign my crown? No I was not ready. I wanted to be in charge of my own destiny.

I decided to 'put God on hold' perhaps until I was old and grey.

It was a watershed moment. I had discovered boys. I searched my heart. Did I really want to give all of myself to God? Yes, I wanted everything He could give to me but for me to give Him anything, least of all my entire life, my ambitions, my selfish desires. No, I was not ready. How could I trust this God I only vaguely knew? He might want me to become a nun or a single missionary like Gladys Aylward. No, I was not ready.

I turned my back on God, on Mary, the Young Peoples Mission and church. I left for "a far country."

Chapter 2

DOING IT MY WAY

At fourteen I called myself an agnostic, mostly because I thought it made me seem sophisticated. I walked away from the love of God. I did not realize it then but He never walked away from me.

Aged seventeen in the sixth form, the big question was what on earth am I supposed to do with my life? I had no clue. It was then that I remembered God. I would try to "keep well in with Him." I would deign to ask Him what He thought I should do. I had not prayed for years. Rather tentatively I said:

"Lord what do you want me to do with my life?"

To my astonishment He answered immediately. I heard Him loud and clear.

"Be a nurse."

I was surprised and delighted. I was quite bookish and not at all practical. (I never even made my own bed). But the idea pleased me. At the time my father was in hospital having had an accident. As I visited him he would eulogize the nurses.

"They are angels," he would often say.

The idea amused me. I would be an angel! I would stroke fevered brows and do GREAT THINGS for humanity. I would be a second Florence Nightingale.

My parents were pleased but when I told my friends they fell about laughing. The father of my current beau was the director of a large mental hospital. He was decidedly unimpressed. Standing tall over six foot high, he regarded me with scorn.

"You! You'll never make a nurse. I'll give you six months."

He was right of course as I was soon to discover. I had been sheltered and pampered. I was not at all practical. I was seriously immature and totally ill-equipped to deal with issues of life and death, and sheer hard work. We were required to be up at 6 am, and more often than not, worked until 9pm with a short break in the afternoon. The average nurse then would walk fifteen miles every day.

At home I had been treated like a child. Now I was expected to function as a capable mature adult. No one swore in my family. No one raised their voice. The hospital is a good place to learn to swear and worse to blaspheme. I learned.

I hated nursing but then so did some of my friends; we formed an anarchic camaraderie. It helped, but most of all it was "I'll give you six months" that rang constantly in my ears.

"I'll show him," I promised myself grimly. "I'll get my State Registration and then I'm out of here."

Nursing was a baptism of fire. Having sailed through exams with little effort I now felt totally out of my depth; being responsible for adults two or three times my age intimidated me. One night attending to a patient in uraemic failure I accidently knocked over his drip sending it crashing to the floor. The entire contents spilled out. This was his lifeline. A taxi had to be sent to bring the emergency pharmacologist to quickly make a replacement. I was devastated. I thought, probably wrongly, that I could have killed him.

Worse than that I began to be tormented by thoughts of death. Aged eighteen I had never known anyone who had died. Now death was everywhere. Many of the people I saw dead or dying were my own age. This was the era of no motorcycle helmets. Literally scores of young men were rushed through our doors with the most appalling injuries; many did not recover.

Laying out the dead bodies of young men was an agonizing experience. I kept asking myself where will they end up? I watched one man slowly dying of cancer of the stomach. His name was Thomas Maloney. He had the most beautiful brown eyes. These eyes would follow me as I passed his bed; those eyes silently implored me, "Help me! Comfort me!" I thought I should tell him about Jesus but then I counteracted the thought with, "Well, I don't believe all that stuff anyway." Even as I thought the words my heart smote me and silently informed me, ***"Yes you do."*** Thomas Maloney endured a slow and painful death. And still I said nothing.

After that incident I became seriously disturbed. Thoughts of death and dying haunted me. What if I were to die? Where would I end up? I knew what the answer was. I would end up in hell. I came under deep conviction – conviction of sin. By now I had learned to swear, worse, to blaspheme. I used the name of God quite frequently, not in reverence and awe, but as an explicative. I worried that I had committed the unpardonable sin. By the time I was twenty one, I was living a fake life. During the day apparently perfectly in control, by night a nervous wreck. I was so afraid of dying that I could not sleep. It was the time of the Suez Crisis and the possibility of a third world war. Every time a plane flew low, to me it signaled nuclear holocaust. I had horrible, tormenting nightmares, frightening dreams of everlasting fire and destruction. I now took pills to sleep and then more pills to get me through the day. I told no one of my distress. Outwardly I was 'just fine.' I was living a lie. My life was unraveling; I became desperate.

I knew I had to do something. I knew I had to find a way back to God. But here the dilemma increased. Would He allow me back into His Presence? I worried that I had committed the unpardonable sin. I had known the truth. I had known His love and forgiveness. Yet deliberately, willfully I had turned my back on Him to live a life entirely for my own pleasure.

I had another worry too. It was the Christians. Those I had observed seemed a sorry, joyless group. In those days most serious Christians wore no makeup, wore dowdy clothes. They did not do a lot of things. They did not go to the cinema, nor did they dance, smoke or drink. What DID they do I wondered? Is Christianity all about not doing things?

Home had become my refuge, my safe place. I would return there whenever my off duty would allow. Often returning on the train back to dreaded hospital I would weep silently regretting the confident, happy go lucky self I used to be.

In this state on Easter Sunday 1959 I made a decision. I would go back to The Young People's Mission. It had now become a church. I would throw myself on God's mercy. I would beg Him for forgiveness and once again I would join the ranks of Christians even if it meant a life of "DON'T DO and dowdy clothes. I was wearing a black leather coat. I slid into the back row hoping no one would recognize me. What I did not know was that this was a special weekend. The preacher was none other than Ian Paisley MP, probably the most powerful speaker I have ever heard. His words were literally like missiles. It felt as if I was being hit in the chest with bricks. He pulled no punches.

"The wages of sin is death," he began

"But the free gift of God is eternal life through the Lord Jesus Christ."

"You are all sinners." I had to agree. Most certainly I was, no contest.

"You are all going to hell." Again I agreed. "You need to repent" Yes.

"All you that want to repent raise your hands."

I folded my arms as tightly as I could. But he would not stop. Several people made their way to the front of the church. Eventually, on perhaps his fourth appeal I gingerly raised my hand.

Before I knew it an eagle eyed usher escorted me to the front. Altogether there were seventeen of us. We were led in a prayer of repentance. I said it, but I was so confused I'm not sure it registered.

Standing at the front, a battle was raging. My thoughts churned round like an out of control spin dryer.

"You don't want to be a Christian. Look at them, they are so dowdy. Then, if you get too close to God He might want you to be a nun."

"But I'm longing for, yearning for peace with God."

I felt like a rope in a tug of war; a team of strong men pulling me towards God, another equally strong team pulling me away.

The next thing I knew was that we were taken away to be counselled. I found myself in a small room with a young woman. She was fresh faced and earnest.

Before she could say anything, all my pent up confusion erupted.

"Listen," I said. "I don't want to be a Christian. You are all fuddy duddies, I don't want to stop going to the cinema. I don't want to stop dancing. I don't want..."

She looked astonished. Before I could continue, she told me. "I'm going to get some help."

With that she fled!

Now I was the one who was wrong footed. All these things were coming out of my mouth but my heart was crying out. It said something totally different.

My heart cried out to God.

"Oh GOD PLEASE don't cast me off! Please don't allow me to go to hell. I know you can never love me, but please just tolerate me. Allow me into Your Kingdom. You don't even have to look in my direction. Just put me at the back. I won't trouble you."

Looking back these words seem astonishing but that is what I said and what I thought.

I was about to have the most seminal moment of my life.

There, alone in that small room. The God of all flesh, the Creator of the Universe spoke to me.

"Kate!" He knew my name! I was extremely afraid. I felt that He would now give me a long list of my sins. I knew that "God is angry with the sinner every day." I stiffened – wait for it...

"I love you."

I was dumbfounded - Almighty, all knowing God love me?

That was the last thing I had expected to hear. I could not take it in.

"No, You can't love me."

Again, **"Kate I love you."**

"No, I hate myself. I'm horrible."

"Kate I love you."

With that there in that small room His love descended upon me enfolding me in a warm blanket of forgiveness. I was saturated in love. My tears flowed freely, tear of relief, tears of gratitude. I was filled with inexpressible joy.

"O Lord," I blurted out," if You love me I'll do anything. I'll go anywhere."

I was "born again" into the family of God.[1]

I walked out of church that day a brand new person.[2]

I was bubbling with joy and relief. I never had another nightmare. In fact I felt like a different person. If God so loved me, I had no need to act, no need to impress anyone. To my surprise I began to enjoy nursing, so much so that I completed the SRN and went on to become a State Registered Midwife. All fear of death left. But perhaps the most amazing discovery was I could be myself. I did not have to be dull or dowdy. This is what I had instinctively rebelled against. Jesus is the most effervescent, charismatic person whoever walked this earth. He was the friend of sinners. He set people free. That day I too was set free. I was LOVED! Love is powerful, indeed it sets us free.[3]

That day I knew I was "accepted in the beloved."[4]

That love is life transforming. The only Person I need to conform to is Jesus. I was free to be myself; the self God created me to be. As St Augustine said, "Love God and do as you please." Anyone who truly loves God will only do what truly pleases Him.

Less than three years later I was in the Bible College of Wales training to be a missionary.

1. *"He came unto His own and His own did not receive Him. But to as many as received Him, to them He gave the right to become children of God, to those who believe on His name: who were born, not of blood, nor of the will of the flesh, nor of the will of man, BUT OF GOD"* **(John 1:11-13).**

2. *"If anyone is in Christ he is a NEW CREATION; old things have passed away; behold, ALL things have become new"* **(2 Corinthians 5:17).**

3. *"If the Son shall set you free, you shall be free indeed"* **(John 8:36).**

4. *"Blessed be the God and Father of our Lord Jesus Christ, who has blessed us with all spiritual blessing in the heavenly places in Christ, just as He CHOSE us in Him before the foundation of the world, the we should be holy and without blame before Him in love, having predestined us to adoption as sons by Christ Jesus to Himself, according to the good pleasure of His will, to the praise of the glory of His grace, by which HE HAS MADE US ACCEPTED IN THE BELOVED"* **(Ephesians 1:3-6).**

Part 2

MAKE ME WILLING NOT TO MARRY

Chapter 3
BIBLECOLLEGE

***"For the eyes of the Lord run to and fro throughout the whole earth, to show Himself strong on behalf of those whose heart is loyal (perfect) towards Him"* (2 Chronicles 16:9).**

I would describe my experience in that upper room as a radical, dynamic, life changing encounter with God, the Father. Now at the Bible College I would have more radical encounters, firstly with the Lord Jesus Christ and later with the Holy Spirit.

After my conversion I set myself on a search. The search was to find someone as dynamic as Jesus. Someone I could follow. One day I met him, George Verwer, the founder of Operation Mobilisation. This extraordinary young man, just one year my senior, was intent on reaching the world for Jesus. Over sixty years later he is still doing just that. In 1961, he had a massive map of Europe and a vision for teams of young people to volunteer one month or more to visit every single home with the good news of salvation through Jesus Christ. Like Ian Paisley, he too was a challenging and effective preacher. I listened transfixed as he spoke of a life of sacrifice and adventure, a life of leaving all and trusting God for all one's needs.

His challenge was, ***"If anyone desires to come after Me, let him deny himself, and take up his cross daily, and follow Me. For whoever desires to save his life will lose it, but whoever loses his life for MY sake will save it. For what profit is it to a man if he gains the whole world, but is himself destroyed or lost? For whoever is ashamed of Me and My words, of him will the Son of Man be ashamed when He comes in His glory."***[1]

I was ready. I had resigned my job. I was waiting to do something for the Lord.

I stood to my feet and volunteered to go to France.

Operation Mobilisation was one of the most exciting and life changing seasons of my life. I volunteered for one month but stayed for three. The team I joined consisted of some twenty five young people, many of them from America. Our remit was to knock on every door of every village in the Bordeaux region. We lived by faith. Each and every day we prayed for a place to sleep and our very ancient bus to function. We sold La Sainte Bible and Billy Graham's Paix avec Dieu (Peace with God). Many of the people we visited had never even seen a Bible as it was only permitted for the priests. The money we gained through our salesmanship provided for our food. (We became very effective!) We had our sleeping bags and slept mostly on hard floors; either the Curé (Priest) would allow us to sleep in the church or the mayor would find us somewhere. I loved every moment of it especially the sense of adventure and the team camaraderie. Four members of the team were BCW (Bible College of Wales) graduates.

"You should go there," they urged.

So it was that I found myself in Swansea after a quick visit home to pick up some things. One of those "things" was a 'kneeler.' This was something to kneel upon! Most evenings at the college there was prayer and if you didn't want to get 'camel's knees' after four hours of intercession, this piece of equipment was essential.

The Bible College was a huge surprise to this rather worldly new Christian. It has been described as a cross between an army boot camp and a monastery. The staff were deeply spiritual. They lived "by faith" and they lived to pray. Rees Howells[2], a miner, who had been deeply impacted by the Welsh Revival of 1904, had founded the College. In my time, the principal was Dr. Samuel Howells, the only son of his more famous father. "Mr. Samuel" as he was known, carried the college by intercession. We students could often see him striding up and down in the grounds, face heavenward agonizing in prayer.

The ethos of the college was both simple and challenging. "If you want to know God, give away all your money and trust Him to provide for all your needs. Learn how to pray to your Father ***'in secret so***

that He can reward you openly.'" The thinking was if you want to trust God for revival, and for many people to give their lives to Christ, start by trusting God for your personal needs and find out just how strong your faith is. Learning faith did not come easily but I thank God for this training, which to this day informs and impacts me.

However, to this uninformed and 'rookie' Christian the ethos and life style was a total shock. Not only was I aghast by what I found but also the college staff were shocked by me. There were strict rules regarding the segregation of the sexes. Of those many rules, the most famous of all, the butt of many jokes, was RULE 8. This stated that on no account should male and female students interact. It was a small campus with just twenty five male students and twenty five females. Although we took lectures every day together, we were not encouraged to fraternize in any way. Not surprisingly, in the 'attraction of the unobtainable,' many students did eventually marry. So much so that among us students, the college had a new title, 'The Bridal College of Wales.'

In addition, the wearing of makeup and fancy clothes was frowned upon. So, when I arrived in my smart suede suit, chunky amber jewellery, plenteous make up with a young man and a sports car in tow, there was consternation all round. We were quickly separated. John was marched off to the men's dining room while I was left, somewhat deflated, waiting for a place with the women. Second shock - the men and women had separate dining rooms.

Not unsurprisingly that was the last I heard from John! I had chattered endlessly about my newfound faith and all the answers to prayer I had experienced in France. He obviously thought I had gone totally overboard and the otherworldly staff and our strange reception must have convinced him to sever the relationship. (We had been good friends, nothing more).

There were more shocks to follow. No one had mentioned to me that we slept in dormitories. I was put into The Ark along with six other young ladies. We were a motely bunch: Eva from Switzerland, Marie from Northern Ireland, Carol from Liverpool, Gwen from the East End of London, Ella from Scotland and me. The seventh occupant was Maureen, newly married and required to live separately from her husband as no married accommodation was on offer. We all slept to the sound of her muffled sobs. Our day started at 6 am to the sound of a grating alarm. That was for our quiet time (something new to me!) Then, to my horror, we were then required to carry out one hour of manual work before breakfast. Each morning I found myself on my hands and knees polishing the already polished parquet floor in the 'Big House' where Mr. Samuel our principal resided.

I was not pleased, "I did not come here to polish floors," I protested. "I came to learn about the Bible."

How wrong I was. The Holy Spirit sent me to this Missionary Training College to learn about myself and to fall in love with Jesus.

And learn about myself I did. I discovered that I was proud, arrogant, opinionated and selfish. And I discovered afresh that God's love necessitates a life of sacrifice and discipline.

So, it was not too long before I gave away what money and jewellery I had, distributed my fashionable clothes, dumped the make-up and began a new adventure of faith and trust in God.

I was quite pleased with myself. I was settling in. I felt I had made huge sacrifices and that God must be quite pleased with me. I walked with a spring in my step, head held high. I acquired a new name, Kangaroo Kate.

I thought I was doing well, but I was in for yet another shock.

1. Luke 9:23–26

2. Rees Howells Intercessor by Norman Grubb

Chapter 4
A SHOCKING QUESTION

***"Take your son, your only son Isaac, whom you love, and go to Mount Moriah and offer him there as a burnt offering"* (Genesis 22:2).**

The voice was loud and clear but surely, I must have been mistaken. I was sitting in the lecture room. It was November; outside the leaves drifted lazily downward in the bright autumn sunshine. I had been awed by the story of the life of Abraham as narrated by Dr. Symmonds. We had reached the sacrifice of Isaac; the three-day journey to Mount Moriah, the wood, the fire and the knife and now – the binding of Isaac, the only son, on the altar. "God can ask of us some very bizarre things," Doc Symmonds was intoning. "We all know that He forbids human sacrifice as abhorrent, yet, here He is asking Abraham to kill the son of promise." "It may be," he continued, "It just maybe, that God is asking something deeply sacrificial of you. What is the thing most dear to you?' Immediately my mind responded, "I want to be married. I want a gorgeous, handsome, fully Christian man."

In fact, one of my greatest excitements about coming to the college was that here I would find THE MAN OF MY DREAMS all neatly packaged, and that together we would sail away to do GREAT EXPLOITS for God. On arriving I had given all the male students a quick appraisal. To my dismay, none of them met my exacting standards; there was one who looked extremely interesting (and dashing), but he was quickly dismissed as 'the wrong colour.'

Back in the classroom there was no remission. Again, we were asked, "What is God asking of you?" Horror gripped me. Everything within me cried out, "No! No! You can't ask that." Silence. No reply.

As soon as the lecture ended, I rushed out into the garden. Walking round and round I presented my case to God. I began with a whine. "That's not fair, "I told my Maker. "That's just too much. Here I am serving You at this college. I've given up my career. I've given away all my money." (I did not have much.) I've given away all my expensive clothes and all my jewellery and now You are asking me never to marry – to be single and celibate all my life. I'm still a virgin. I've been waiting for the right man and now You say there is to be no-one."

Silence.

I tried again. "Look, You know me. I like men. I've kept myself but I've got hormones and You know I'd love to have children."

Silence. There was no answer. It seemed as if God had left me.

It was a miserable week. I spent most of it whining. "You shouldn't ask me this. It's not fair."

And still the silence. How I missed the sweet presence of the Holy Spirit.

Salvation came on Thursday evening in the shape of a visiting speaker. The college was first and foremost a missionary training institution and we frequently hosted missionaries from various parts of the globe. I cannot remember the name of the speaker but what he said transformed my life. This is what he told us:

"There may be times when the Lord will ask you something so hard that you simply cannot find it within you to say "Yes" to Him. In those situations, here is a prayer:

"Make me willing to be willing."

Light was dawning. Hope rose up. I clutched at this statement like a drowning man would grasp a life jacket. That night in the room I shared, I knelt by my bed. "O Lord, You know how much I wanted to marry. You know how I would love to have children but if Your plan is for me to single and celibate all my life – make me willing to be willing."

That was it. Suddenly it seemed easy. My prayer was heard. Immediately I knew the presence of the Holy Spirit. I was filled with joy; even with relief. So, I was going to be single! No problem. I could (and did) forget about men. All desire for marriage and children left. I was free to get on with my life. More importantly I was free to seek a deeper walk with God with no distractions.

The first year passed. I learned a lot. The college was an extraordinary place populated by extraordinary people. Most of the staff were in their fifties and sixties. They seemed very old, very wise and they led challenging and exemplary lives. Many of them had been young students during the Second World War; they had been led by a man who laid down his life in prayer, Rees Howells. One fateful day in 1942, just before the Battle of Britain, when Hitler was poised to invade and conquer the land. Rees had announced, *"Prayer has failed. Intercession must take over."* He now challenged the students to make a vow of celibacy as an act of intercession. Many did so. Not only was the entire college praying at that time but King George V1 called the whole nation to days of prayer. Although Hitler was well prepared to invade, inexplicably against all odds, the planned invasion of Great Britain failed to materialize and the progress of victory for the allies began. God heard. Our nation was saved through prayer.

After the war instead of going on to the mission field, many of the students choose to stay in Wales and live a life of complete dependence on God. They not only prayed for their own needs, but sent thousands of pounds monthly to missionaries.

I was happy in this new environment. It was so stimulating to 'pray to my Father in secret so that He could reward me openly.' I was having adventures in faith. The first thing I prayed for was a tube of toothpaste. I felt highly embarrassed to talk to the Creator of the universe, the One who holds the planets and galaxies in His hand, about toothpaste. I felt He had enough to do without my little request.

However just two days after asking, as I prepared for bed, I lifted my pillow, and to my astonishment and delight, found a TUBE OF TOOTHPASTE hidden underneath. To this day I revel in the wonder of that moment; that an Almighty God could show such infinite care for me. There were many other things to pray for too, including the £25 needed each term for our fees, fares home, toiletries and gifts. Little by little I was learning the life of total dependence on a loving Heavenly Father. Once, walking in the rain I found a £1 note. I took it back, washed it and thanked my God!

Apart from my personal needs, I was seeing God at work in more important ways. There was a crisis in the Belgian Congo and every night, prayer was made for the missionaries and Christians there. Many were massacred. We heard that one of our ex-students was with a group of missionaries, hiding of all places, in a brewery; hostile Simbas surrounded them. We were praying. On the third evening of extended prayer, we suddenly felt we could no longer pray. In fact, prayer turned into praise and rejoicing. Both staff and students knew that we had "got through." Sometime later we learned that a mercenary "Mad Mike Hoare" had driven through the enemy lines burst into the brewery and rescued all who were inside. The time of the rescue was exactly when we began rejoicing in the spirit. Such lessons in prayer cannot be forgotten.

Although life at the college could be tough, I was enjoying every minute of it. The staff were without exception outstandingly godly people. They knew and walked with the Holy Spirit. My favourite lecturer was Ieuan Jones, a gifted Bible expositor. He and his wife had been missionaries in China, though he rarely mentioned it. He seemed to have only one suit. It was navy blue and shone with age - just like his face! I can hear his soft, lilting Welsh voice now as he disclosed profound mysteries to us. Many times, when he finished, we students were unable to move because of the solemn awe of God upon us. We would sit in silence, no one moving.

The evening prayer times were exciting too. Together the staff and students would listen to missionaries from all over the world such as Len Moules, the leader of the World Wide Evangelisation Crusade. Duncan Campbell would tell us of the Hebridean Revival, Samuel Howells on the Welsh Revival, and many others also. After they had shared we would pray as they led us.

I discovered that not only did Samuel Howells trust God for £2,500 it took to keep the college running each month, but in addition he would send a further £2,500 out to various missionaries as the Holy Spirit led. This quiet, gentle, unassuming man was a hero of faith.

Perhaps the most exciting aspect was learning to pray. I had progressed from the toothpaste to money for my fees and daily needs. I had even learned to give money away when I myself was in need. I was learning to love the word of God and the life of faith. More than anything else I wanted to know the Holy Spirit, though I was a little afraid of Him. There were challenges too. It was an international student body with students from many nations and various

Christian backgrounds. Most of my friends were Pentecostals and though I loved their camaraderie, I was deeply suspicious of their strange beliefs. I had ventured into Pentecostal meetings on two occasions. There was a lot of shouting and I was commanded to 'receive.' No, it did not sit well with me. Besides I had been told that to be baptized with the Holy Spirit you might roll on the floor and foam at the mouth!!

So, the year passed and the students ahead of us were due to leave - twenty five of them. It dawned on me that I would never see one of these students again. His name was Paul Jinadu. Of all the second-year students he seemed to me to be the most outstanding. I admired him a lot. I hardly knew him but what I did know, I liked. I felt really sad that we would never meet again but I didn't think too much about it because men were off my agenda.

Two months' vacation loomed ahead; I headed home wondering what I should do.

Chapter 5

YOU PLAYED A TRICK ON ME

***"Because you have not withheld your son, your only son – blessing I will bless you..."* (Genesis 22:16).**

I had not been home long when I received a phone call. It was from Bryan, the husband of my roommate, Maureen. "We are holding a week-long mission in Treorchy," he said, "and we would like you to be part of the team." I had never heard of Treorchy but I agreed to go. I discovered it was a Welsh mining town in the Rhonda Valley.

Probably because it was cheaper, I elected to travel by the overnight train. I arrived, somewhat bleary eyed at 6am. A figure came to meet me; I noticed his smile, then the whites of his eyes. It was Paul Jinadu! My heart began to pound and I was filled with joy.

My favourite male student who I thought had left my life forever was right here on the platform with me. I was flustered. I spoke severely to my fluttering heart. "Stop that! You are not getting married – remember? And anyway, he's the wrong colour."

I calmed down and Paul took me to the family with whom I would stay. They were Doreen and Rhyddid Thomas; they owned a shoe shop on the High Street – a beautiful couple who loved the Lord and who supported the work of the Bible College. To my surprise I found that there were only four of us on the team, Maureen, Bryan, Paul and I.

The very first evening we were witnessing to some young men who were quite drunk. One of them was really taken with Paul and followed him everywhere. Soon he was calling him, "Brother Paul." To which Paul replied, "You are my friend but you can only be my brother if you receive Jesus as your Saviour." With that the guy broke down and prayed to be born again. It was an exciting and busy time. Most days we were on the streets talking to people and in the evenings there were meetings designed to be attractive to young people with music, films and preaching.

We were busy every day but Thursday afternoon was free. I told Paul, "I want to ask you a question."

"That's fine," he said. "And I have a question for you too."

We took a stroll up the hillside overlooking the town. My question was about the Person of the Holy Spirit and how did speaking in tongues fit in. The answer was very long but at the end I was happy. By now we had descended and were standing beside the main road.

"Thanks so much, "I said. "Now I know what I'm going to do."

"What about my question?" he replied.

"Yes, what is it?" (I was in a hurry to go.)

His question was a bolt from the blue, "Will you marry me?"

I was dumbfounded. My mind was racing. It seemed as if a million thoughts were swirling round. The first went like this, "Lord I thought he was spiritual. If he was really in tune with You, he would know I'm not getting married." My second thought - complete astonishment! It was as if a spiritual giant was approaching a spiritual pigmy. Then there was some delight. "Fancy him asking me!" Followed by "Lord, how do I get out of this? Has he forgotten we are not the same colour?" Remember this was 1964; the time of apartheid. In the sleepy town where I was raised, there were no foreigners. I had never heard of a mixed marriage. Furthermore, though I had wonderful loving parents, racial prejudice was rife in our home.

I had to get away. "Excuse me," I blurted out, "I have to go." With that I took off and ran. I was thoroughly shaken.

My mind was still in turmoil. "Lord," I cried, "Do you allow this? Is it OK for black and white to mix?"

I ran up the stairs to the Thomas's prayer room. They had a huge map of the world on the wall with the pictures of all the missionaries they prayed for. There right in the middle was a picture of a West Indian lady together with an English looking man. Underneath was the caption, "Mr. and Mrs. John Smith serving God in Jamaica." I was astonished.

I had plenty more to say: "Lord, I hardly know him. Lord, I don't love him."

Sometimes our God is funny. He laughs! It was as if He said, "Well let's talk about this, shall we. Remember the first time you saw him, you thought that he exactly fitted the bill for you except that (to quote) "He is the wrong colour." Then you dismissed him. Remember how when he was leaving, you were incredibly sad. Remember when you saw him on the station platform your heart leapt for joy?" The Lord continued, "You like him, you respect him, you admire him and you like to be near him. Kate, you did not recognize it. You shut down your sexuality, but Kate this is love. You love him."

"But Lord," I countered. "You said I should never marry."

"Kate, I did not say 'you should never marry' I asked if you are you willing never to marry."

"Lord, You played a trick on me."

Chapter 6

MAY I HAVE AN ANSWER?

The man I eventually married is so different to me. He is a hare while I am a tortoise. Once he hears from God, the firing gun has started and he is off at a hundred miles an hour. Me – I weigh things. I look, consider, examine, ponder, look for evidence it's a lengthy process. So, when the following day he asked me for my answer all I could say was, "Give me time. Don't contact me. Let me hear from God."

As it happened there was very little opportunity for further contact. Immediately after the Treorchy outreach, Paul headed off to Scotland to join The Faith Mission while I was soon back at Swansea for my second college year.

While suddenly I was excited about the prospect of marrying this amazing man, I had several hurdles to surmount. First and foremost, I needed to know for sure that it was God's will. Having got used to the idea of singleness I now had to re-evaluate. Then there was parental consent. I was sure they would never support such a union.

I went before the Lord. "Father do you really approve of mixed marriages?" The answer came quickly as I read through the book of Acts, where I read in chapter 17, verse 26 that (God) has made all nations of one blood." And in Galatians chapter 3 verse 26 which says:

"In Christ there is neither Jew nor Greek, neither slave nor free, there is neither male nor female: for we are all one in Christ Jesus."

So, God allows it, but does He want it for me? That was my next question. I decided to ask for a sign. "Lord I'm asking that if this is Your will, all my fees will be paid before the end of October." Living by faith is not easy. I had found it quite difficult to pray in the amount needed for each term. Just one week after this prayer I discovered four letters in my pigeonhole. I opened them with growing excitement. Each had a sum of money in them and together, they made up the exact amount I needed.

I sat down and wrote, "The answer is Yes."

The second obstacle I needed to address was the baptism of the Holy Spirit. Everyone in the college knew that my husband to be spoke in tongues according to the words of Jesus in Acts chapter one verse eight, ***"You shall receive power when the Holy Spirit has come upon you and you shall be witnesses unto Me..."***

Somewhat reluctantly I accompanied my friends Sandra and Rhoda to a Pentecostal lady, Auntie Jeanie who was to pray for me. And pray for me they did, hard and long. Nothing happened. They were dispirited so took off to the kitchen to comfort themselves with a good old cup of tea! Meanwhile I stayed on my knees and prayed a funny prayer. It went like this, "O Lord please fill me with the Holy Spirit even if I roll on the floor, or worse foam at the mouth." Suddenly a fountain of joy was released deep within I began to laugh and laugh and laugh. This is NOT what I had expected. I had never heard anyone laugh in church! And here I was gurgling with joy nonstop. My laughter alerted my praying friends. "You have been filled with the Spirit," they declared. It certainly was a wonderful experience and as I rose from my knees I heard myself say, "O Jesus I love You." It was as if before I had known about Him, now I KNEW Him in a deep and more intimate way. Sometime later I received the "angel language"[1] enabling me to speak in languages I have never learned. This gift was extremely useful many years later when I was confronted by an armed gang. (I escaped!)

I was elated. I was going to marry Paul Jinadu. I thought my heart would burst. But there was a third hurdle to overcome. I knew my parents would not approve. So, I kept this secret to myself. I told no one. I felt that my parents should be the first to know and that before telling anyone we should ask for their permission.

My parents were wonderful people but they could not understand what had happened to their daughter. They even suspected that I was in a cult. Why else would I leave a good job, give away most of my possessions and go to that 'funny place.' Why go to such a strange place to get a diploma when I could have gone to university and come out with a degree in theology? As for living by faith, "no daughter of mine shall be a beggar," my father had declared.

In order to allay their fears, I had invited them to come and stay and see for themselves. They came. They were impressed but still mystified by this 'religious' daughter.

During the Christmas vacation I broke the news that a fellow student wanted to marry me. He was an African from Nigeria and he was black!

As I had feared they were distraught. Over the next eighteen months, we had meetings upon meetings but they were adamant. There was no way they would give their blessing. And indeed they never did. Eventually, regretfully we were married without their blessing and without any of my family. While from Paul's family blessings abounded.

I learned a lot during those eighteen months. I learned that I had been forgiven much, therefore I too, could forgive. When I was accused and misunderstood I learned to bless. When we made known our intent to marry many people were appalled including some quite famous clergymen my mother invited to tell me the error of my ways. At college one member of staff said, "Satan has appeared as an angel of light." An intercessor wrote, "I am praying against this marriage every day." My aunt told me, "You are destroying this family. You are a wicked woman."

Just two weeks before the wedding my mother said she would have a break down. I should abandon the marriage. I was in a dilemma. I loved my parents and didn't want to hurt them. Yet at the same time I could clearly see that the only thing stopping our marriage was racial prejudice. Did I capitulate or hold my ground? One thing the Lord clearly told me was that I should not condemn anyone or disrespect them.

"Its racial prejudice and you had plenty of it, so don't you dare judge anyone who is judging you."

I walked into a church to pray. I knelt down. I asked the Lord "Why can't we go back to plan A? You asked me not to marry. I was cool with that. This wedding is upsetting everyone. Let me call it off."

I love the Lord. He never forces. He replied,

"You can call it off if you like but you will be missing My best plan for your life."

Something else was worrying me.

"What if they all are right and I'm making a mistake? That would be catastrophic."

In front of me there was a beautiful stain glass window. Written on it were these words,

***"Now unto Him who is able to keep you from falling and to present you faultless in the presence of His glory with exceeding joy, To the only wise God, our Saviour, be glory and majesty, dominion and power, both now and forever. Amen"* (Jude 24).**

My Father, God spoke to me.

"Kate you really love Me?"

"Yes."

"You would do anything for Me?"

"Yes."

"Do you seriously think that with your life in My hands I will allow you to do the wrong thing?"

Strengthened, I left the church and told my parents that much as I loved them I would still marry Paul.

My mother asked me to pack my things and leave.

If not to marry was hard, paradoxically now 'to marry' was even harder.

1. *"Though I speak with the tongues of men and of angels, but have not love, I have become sounding brass or a clanging cymbal"* **(1 Corinthians 13:1).**

Chapter 7

FOUR DAYS BEFORE THE WEDDING

I left my parents' home clutching my suitcase. Shortly after our decision to go ahead, the Lord had given us a promise,

"Behold I send an Angel before you to keep you in the way and to bring you into the place which I have prepared" **(Exodus 23:20)**.

We had intended to move in after our marriage but here I was four days early. The "prepared place" was 137 East Parade, York, less than ten minutes' walk from the home of my parents. It was an elegant terraced Edwardian period house with four bedrooms and two reception rooms. It even had a garden with small orchard. It was not only fully furnished but there was bed linen, china, a piano and lots of Christian books. We had none of these luxuries; we were amazed at the kindness of the owners and the goodness of our God. All this was ours for the princely sum of £4 a month!

The owners, Joan and Ian Bull were formerly the curates of the Anglican Church right across the road.

(The very church I attended as a young girl.) They had left Britain to be missionaries in South America. Before leaving they had attempted to put the house on the market. As they entered the offices of the Estate Agent, they distinctly heard a Voice saying,

"Do not do anything with the house. I have people who need it." Noticing that it was empty I sent a telegram to them asking if it was available. We quickly had a reply: THE HOUSE IS YOURS USE EVERYTHING IN IT.

My husband to be was in Scotland working with the Faith Mission. He travelled to York the day before our wedding to prepare for the arrival of his sister and her family and his cousins.

So it was that I spent three days in the house entirely alone – but not alone!

Almost the first thing I did was to get out my handkerchief, my Bible and get on my knees. I began to weep my way through the Psalms. When I got to Psalm 27 I was "arrested." The Lord began to speak to me so beautifully, so powerfully. The psalmist is King David. He had been anointed King but not enjoying any of the glory. He was running for his life, hiding from King Saul who attempted fifteen times to kill him. At the time of writing, he was holed up in a cave surrounded by 3,000 men. There was no way of escape. Yet he wrote these words:

"The Lord is my light and my salvation
Whom shall I fear?
The Lord is the strength of my life,
Of whom shall I be afraid?
Though an army encamp against me,
My heart shall not fear:
Though war may rise against me,
In this will I be confident
One thing I have desired of the Lord,
That will I seek:
That I may dwell in the house of the Lord
All the days of my life,
To behold the beauty of the Lord,
And to inquire in His temple."

The Holy Spirit stopped me right there and began to speak. He told me not to worry about the chaos and distress our marriage was causing. He told me not to fret nor to apportion blame. I should keep loving and blessing my parents and everyone else who was causing us heartache. I should do what David did in his great trouble; ignore the pain and gaze on the beauty of the Lord Jesus Christ. It is hard for me to describe the profound revelation that came to me then. I can only say that it changed my life.

I have discovered if one can always keep one's eyes on Jesus in every situation He will bring peace and calm even in the midst of the storm. As I meditated on the verses, the Lord came to me. He came to David too for a message came to Saul that the Philistines were attacking Israel so he quickly withdrew his 3,000 men and yet again David escaped.

Later in the Psalm I read rather poignantly,

"When my father and mother forsake me,
Then the Lord will take care of me."

I was comforted but I continued to read. Another breakthrough came in Psalm 45 – the Wedding Psalm. In my Bible it is titled: The Glories of the Messiah and His Bride. The psalm divides neatly into two; the first half describes the glorious bridegroom and the second His bride. Again the Lord spoke to me: verse 10 &11;

"Listen, O daughter,
Consider and incline your ear;
Forget your own people also, and your father's house
So the King will greatly desire your beauty:
Because He is your Lord, worship Him."

Then verse 16,

"Instead of your fathers shall be your sons
Whom you will make princes in all the earth."

I read and reread these psalms with growing excitement and indeed they have become the key to my life. God was sanctioning our marriage. He was blessing it. Our children would not be "half castes" as people had said. They would be princes! No one had ever called me beautiful but here all alone the One to whom I had given my life was calling me just that – beautiful.

Our marriage is blessed with two sons who love us and love the Lord. They each have beautiful wives and we rejoice in three amazingly talented granddaughters.

As I write today we have been married for fifty-three years. It's been an adventure and as I said, we like adventures.

Chapter 8
OUR WEDDING

***"For this reason a man shall leave his father and mother and cleave to his wife, and they shall become one flesh"* (Genesis 2:25).**

We were married by our pastor, Douglas Greenfield, in the church where I had committed my life to God at the age of eleven and where I had promised to serve Him with all my heart at the age of twenty-one. My earthly father was not there to walk me down the aisle and as I stepped out of the taxi with my Bridesmaid, Sandra I suddenly felt heartbroken. I thought of my sister, Jane. Her beautiful wedding dress was hanging in the wardrobe, next to my sister Lesley's bridesmaid dress. In two months time she would be walking down the aisle on daddy's arm. I could feel the tears welling up. Suddenly I heard a voice from heaven, ***"I am your Father and I will give you to your husband."*** I was filled with joy. I literally pranced down the aisle. All my friends were there and the entire church who put on our wedding reception supported us. Doug preached a wonderful message from Psalm 25:14,

"The secret of the Lord is with them that fear Him Unto such He will show His covenant."

We made our vows before God that we would love each other until "death do us part."

When we returned from honeymoon one week later, who should be waiting to meet us?

My parents came asking for forgiveness. To Paul they said, "You are now our son and we accept you."

Our courtship had mostly been conducted by mail. In one of his letters to me Paul had asked if I could take the attitude of Ruth who told her mother-in-law, Naomi

"Entreat me not to leave you or turn back from following you, for where you go I will go. Where you lodge, I will lodge, your people shall be my people, and your God, my God. Where you die, I will die. The Lord do to me and more also if anything but death separates you and me" **(Ruth 1:16-17).**

I took both promises as vows before God. I did not know that both were to be tested.

Just four months later, we sailed for Lagos to begin our ministry together. While we were there my parents began to attend church and they too committed their lives to Christ. I thank God that throughout this difficult time we never lost our love and respect for them.

Part 3

MAKE ME WILLING TO RETURN TO NIGERIA

Chapter 9

NIGERIA, HERE WE COME

Four months after our wedding, we sailed to Nigeria. It was September 1966. While we were arriving many others were getting out, for this was the start of a bloody and bruising conflict – the Biafra War, which was to last for three dreadful years.

We were young and enthusiastic. It was a big challenge and I have always enjoyed adventures. We carried five suitcases and two hundred pounds. I also carried a 'little secret.' I was two months pregnant. We were idealists. We had very little idea of what we would do except, of course, to win the world for Jesus. Paul had left Nigeria exactly ten years before when he was just fourteen. He had left as a staunch Moslem educated in the Koranic School, praying five times daily and with the ambition to go to Mecca. Now he was returning as a Christian with a completely different outlook but with absolutely no knowledge of the Christian life of Nigeria.

He was also returning in disgrace. Not only had he renounced Islam, the religion of his forefathers, but he had also eschewed a medical career. His amazing mother had paid for his private education and he was just about to enter medical school when he had experienced a life-changing encounter with the Risen Lord. Jesus had appeared to him. He had shown him His nailed pierced hands and melted Paul's heart with His love. From that moment, my husband had only one desire and that was to tell everyone he could that there is only one way to God and that is through the Lord Jesus Christ. To return to Nigeria with no degree, no prestige and little money did not fill *Mama Agba's* heart with joy; she had spent a huge amount of money to educate her children and in her view, it had all been wasted. She now spent a lot of energy trying to make her son 'respectable.' If he must be a preacher, he could be a high Anglican or better still, work for Radio Nigeria. She had influence. She would pull strings. She meant well and was extremely kind to me, but soon we escaped from her clutches by joining a Christian church where Paul was employed as an evangelist.

Though this move had seemed to us to be God's will, for me it was a baptism of fire. I have to confess I was never happy in this church. When we agreed to join, we had been entirely won over by the gentle, godly General Overseer. We had never attended a service and when we joined the congregation, their services seemed interminable; they were conducted in Yoruba, a language I did not yet understand. The women sat on one side and were supposed to keep silent while our husbands and sons sat aloof from the crying babies and all the detritus of the female kind. The beautiful leader of the church was entirely eclipsed by The Prophet, who ruled with a rod of iron. In the years we were there, I never felt the presence of the Holy Spirit.

This church strongly believed in divine healing and we were told that it was founded on miracles. These miraculous healings were so impressive that it was decreed that taking medicine was a sin and definitely not an option open to members. Although intellectually we could not subscribe to this doctrine we nevertheless obeyed, and if my memory serves me correctly, we took no malaria prophylactics in a high malaria zone.

However, salvation was at hand. We were soon discovered by university undergraduates and school children. In an age where nearly all the clergy were over 55 (retirement age) we were definitely different. We were young, we were educated and we were a 'mixed' marriage. Invitations to the top schools and universities came pouring in. We were astonished by the response to the simple preaching of the good news. Entire classes of children and students would pray to receive Christ as their Saviour. These meetings were wonderful.

That was the good news – the not so good news was that I was struggling to adjust. I vomited throughout the pregnancy. The only thing I could tolerate was Bournvita. It was my lifeline. Philip is a Bournvita baby. To this day I love it. I left England weighing nine stone, and by the time Philip was born, I was down to seven. Many people did not even know that I was carrying a baby. The actual birth was badly managed and extremely traumatic. I still can't talk about it.

I was lonely too. After the birth, how I longed for my mother but she was 3,000 miles away. When Philip was three months old, we had a horrid shock. A girl in the flat below us also had a baby. On this particular day, I greeted her in the morning and observed the baby on her back. That evening there was a dreadful wailing. We learned that the baby had died. This death frightened me. I would watch Philip for hours to ensure that he was breathing. It was then we took the decision that although we would not take medicines, our son would always have his 'Sunday-Sunday' prophylactic.

By the second year of our stay 'Brother Paul' had become quite well known. It was then that the prophet issued a decree. My husband was to visit all thirty two churches in the Lagos area for revival meetings. He was to prepare for one week, preach for one week and do follow up and rest for the third week before moving to the next venue. We started; almost immediately, amazing things began to happen; a lady in a wheelchair was completely healed, a dumb man spoke, a witch who came to deal with Paul was arrested by the Holy Spirit and could not move. The prophet was extremely happy. He now prophesied that Paul should stay in the Lagos Church and preach every night. It was an amazing time; many people were coming to faith in Christ but after sixteen weeks my husband said that he was exhausted and needed a rest. The prophet was not pleased but said we could take a week off.

There is a little island, one mile from the Marina called Tarkwa Bay. We went there carrying Philip in our arms. It seemed like heaven. As we disembarked, my husband said, "I'm ready for this; I'm shaking." He drank some well water. Darkness closed in and he began to be violently ill. All night long he threw up and staggered to the toilet. All night long I knelt by him and prayed. By the morning he was unconscious. Driven by desperation, I ran around holding Philip and begging for help. Fortunately, the first boat arrived at 6am and my husband was carried on to it. Arriving opposite the Cathedral he was unceremoniously dumped on the quay. Wonderfully, we knew the Archbishop's chaplain and his office was directly opposite my moribund spouse. I ran across the road, Philip still in my arms. To my huge relief the chaplain was there. He had a massive Volvo and Paul was bundled in as we made our way to the Lagos Island General Hospital. As he was being admitted my husband briefly regained consciousness. I was distressed, "I'm so sorry but you are in hospital." I had "sinned" in the grossest way by defying the teaching of the church.

Four days and several litres of saline later, he was discharged. "Don't apologize," he said, "You have saved my life." The prophet and the elders were outraged and that was the end of our ministry with that denomination. They mostly blamed the unbelieving English wife.

Paul now concentrated all his efforts on the students' union and university campuses.

We were free! He was also beginning to realize that he was not well equipped to answer some of the theological questions posed by the students. He began to study and after some time asked me if I would like to return to the UK so that he could obtain a Divinity degree.

Would I mind? Would I mind!!!! The thoughts of hot baths, constant electricity, friendship and fellowship in English - Would I mind? I was so excited I thought I would burst.

As I write this I'm overwhelmed with the goodness and grace of God. We returned to England with a young child and a thousand pounds in the bank. (My salary: I had been a teacher.) In the goodness of God, Paul enrolled in the London Bible College for a three-year course. The Lord gave us rent-free accommodation in a vicarage with an acre of grounds. My father suggested that Paul apply for a student grant. We did so, but we were not hopeful. To our astonishment, the head of the York Education Authority gave us a full grant with an allowance for me and our children. (Simon was born in Paul's second year.) The thousand pounds stayed in the bank. (Many years later we were able to buy the very house that the head of the Education Authority had lived in.)

I was still very thin. When my mother saw me, she was aghast. "You look awful," she cried and to anyone we met, "Doesn't she look awful?" I hardly admitted it but I was close to breakdown.

I soon put on weight. Life in England was a doddle. There was no war, no starvation, no cockroaches, no mosquitoes; There was no *wahala*; no interminable queues at the bank. I understood the language and every time I worshipped in my native tongue, rivers of tears flowed down my face. That lasted for a whole year.

The three years passed very happily. Life was a blast. Our two young sons were lively and healthy. In our final year our vicarage accommodation was requisitioned and Paul suggested we use our thousand pounds to put a deposit on a house in York. Better and better, I was now near my parents and school friends. We could worship at the church where we were married and where everyone had been so kind to us. Life could not have been more comfortable. My husband commuted to London while I was happily domestic in York. At weekends, he took up carpentry and made a fitted kitchen and fitted wardrobes while I took up interior décor so that our house was extremely comfortable. Every Wednesday, my friends would come to our house and we would pray 'for the people in Nigeria.'

So the three years passed. My husband was nearing graduation when he announced, "When I've got what we came for, we are going back." It was a bombshell. Everything within me screamed I can't do it. Go back to what? The Unknown? I remembered dressing up with my *buba*, wrapper and *gel*e, and if that was not enough, endeavouring to carry the baby on my back. (It didn't work, he kept slipping out). The gele would slip drunkenly and the wrapper would unwrap! I remembered all the etiquette, the curtseys, the *'e kaaro, se alafia ni.'* I had tried so hard to be the perfect Yoruba wife. I had lost so much weight.

I kept quiet. I would pray that he would change his mind. A thought came, "Maybe he should go and I would stay. Yes, I would stay with the children and pray for him." That sounded like a good idea. I held my peace.

Next weekend he was back and full of plans. We would sell the house. "SELL THE HOUSE?" I screamed inside. We would sell the house and use the money to buy our fares and a car.

My cosy, comfortable world was shattered. When we had travelled out in 1966 it had been a big adventure. But this was different. I now knew exactly what I was going to, and the challenges I would face. I reflected ruefully on the day I put my bare foot in my shoe only to find a live cockroach in it and the night when something ran across my face - a gecko, a mouse? O Lord!

My husband was full of plans. We would go as soon as the house was sold. Meanwhile I was dutifully hosting the weekly prayer meeting to pray for Nigeria. This particular evening, I was praying a long (and I thought) eloquent prayer! In the middle of it, I broke down and started shouting, "Lord I don't want to go. Lord I can't go." That rather upset the prayer meeting. I was weeping with huge wracking sobs.

An older lady came and put her arms round me. I thought she would say, "My precious darling, you have really suffered." Instead she said, "You know what you have to do? You have to die to self." I was not pleased. That was not what I wanted to hear. "What a horrible lady!" I thought. "She doesn't know what it's like out there."

After everyone left, alone with God, I had a huge pity party. "She says I've got to die. She doesn't know anything." I said it a lot ad infinitum. God did not answer.

After a whole week of moaning and banging, I knelt by my bed and prayed the prayer of relinquishment. It went something like this:

"Lord, You know how hard I tried. You know how much I suffered. You know what it's like out there but 'make me willing to be willing.'"

There on my knees, I had the most extraordinary experience. It was as if God came like a Divine Surgeon, slit open my chest, took out my English heart and threw it away. In its place, He gave me a deep love for Nigeria and all things Nigerian. It was as simple as that. ***He then spoke to me. "You tried too hard. You are English. You are not Nigerian. Be yourself. You don't have to wear those clothes if you are not comfortable. You will never be a Nigerian but I am giving you a supernatural love for that land and all its people. I love them and so can you."***

I tell you, God is wonderful. The joy came back. We sold our house. Gave away our stuff and went to live in Ibadan. We lived there for one year then a further four years before returning to York so that our boys could have the best education we could provide. Now we live in London but I am so happy whenever I am in Nigeria. I love and admire the people more than I can say. I love the heat, I love and respect the culture. I feel completely at ease there. The one church we planted has multiplied to over five hundred. We have church plants in many nations. I now co-direct a charity which has a far reaching impact in Nigeria. We have the privilege to work with many truly amazing people who are not just co-workers but our friends, our "sons" and "daughters." We have a huge family.

My husband has blossomed as a Man of God, a man of stature. A man who is highly respected in many nations but most of all he is loved as a father and a role model; most of all to me, his wife.

When God does something, He makes a thorough job. Indeed, His yoke is easy and His burden is light.

Part 4

WHAT IF PERSECUTION SHOULD COME?

Chapter 10
SUFFERING

"Discipleship means allegiance to the suffering Christ, and it is therefore not at all surprising that Christians should be called upon to suffer" Dietrich Bonhoeffer

A fourth serious challenge came to me while we were living in Ibadan and working with the Four Square Gospel Church. The time was June 1978. I was forty years old; our youngest son was seven; Philip aged eleven, had been sent back to England to continue his schooling there. While Paul and I were enjoying our work with the Four Square Church, he was also much in demand as a speaker. However, it was a difficult and dangerous time in Ibadan particularly for female *'oyinbos'* (white, or 'peeled' people!) who were being targeted by a gang who went around robbing and raping. They targeted only white women. One of our friends was a Southern Baptist missionary; a refined and godly lady in her sixties. She had been one of the victims. Her husband had been tied up and locked in the bathroom while she was raped and their home ransacked. All of us who knew them were shocked and appalled.

My husband had been invited to conduct a series of meetings for the Sudan United Mission in Jos. He was to be away from us for three long weeks. There were, of course, no mobile phones then and though our flat boasted a black bakelite phone, it hardly ever worked. We knew there would be no communication between us. So, it was with no little sadness that Simon and I drove him to the airport and watched the fragile six-seater mission plane take off. His last words were, "Always drive with car doors locked and remember to be security conscious." I was miserable. Not only were we to be without him for three long weeks, but it seemed that violence and danger were everywhere around.

I decided Simon and I needed some comfort. It was Saturday. We would have a treat. We would head to the University Staff Club, have a swim, a chicken pie and a can of coke. As an extra special treat, I would purchase The Daily Telegraph. In those days it cost a whole pound; (that was when unbelievably one Naira was equal to one pound sterling).

We reached the poolside and changed into our swimwear. Simon wasted no time in jumping in. I was savouring the moment; I spread out my towel on the sunbed and covered myself liberally with sunscreen and opened the paper. I intended to read it from cover to cover. As I unfolded page one I was hit by a massive banner headline, it screamed:

"NINE MISSIONARIES
MASSACRED IN RHODESIA."

I flipped the pages. The first eight were devoted to this horrifying event. There were pictures; graphic pictures. I read that those who were killed were English missionaries from the Elim Pentecostal Church. One of those killed was from my home town, York. I was deeply distressed. I felt sick. I had to get home. "Simon," I called, "We have to go. Sorry, please get dressed."

Oblivious to his disappointment, we were quickly home. Later that evening when he was safely sleeping, I read through the accounts of nine dreadful deaths. It was not easy reading; I sobbed and sobbed.

Nine adults had been murdered and four children. They were three families, the McCanns, the Evans and the Lynns. Then there were three single ladies, Mary Fisher – a teacher, while Catherine Picken, and Wendy Hamilton-White were both nurses. This small band of workers managed a boy's school and a 70-bed hospital which gave nurture, healing and succour to the people and communities of a remote area of what is now Zimbabwe close to the border with Mozambique.

The killings were brutal in the extreme. The weapons used were axes, bayonets and logs. Peter McCann had been found with his hands tied behind his back. His face and body were covered in stab wounds, and an axe was embedded in his neck. Every other person had been severely beaten and disfigured. Another body, that of Catherine Picken had multiple wounds to the chest and embedded in the back of her head was a long-handled axe. Three young children were found together; Joy and Philip McCann lay face down next to five-year old Rebecca Evans who had nine stabs wounds. Most poignant of all was the youngest victim, just three weeks old. The skull of the much-awaited Pamela Grace Lynn had been crushed by an army boot; the imprint clearly visible.

Each of the women had been raped.

I do not think I have ever been so distressed. Alone there with my own fears I began to shout at God.

"Where were You when all this happened?" I demanded.

"How could You allow this?"

"Who saw who being raped?"

"Did the children witness this?"

"These people left everything to follow You. They were unarmed, defencelesss and doing Your will. Why did You not prevent this carnage?'

And then, "Listen, don't allow anything like that to happen to me. Don't put it on my agenda. I want You to know I'm not willing to die a violent death and I'm definitely not willing to be raped.'

I was on my knees beside myself with grief.

In that moment my God came to me.

There alone in the darkened room I was caught up in a vision. There was thick blackness everywhere. Then I saw an angry sea. There were huge foam-capped breakers some twenty feet high, crashing and rolling with great ferocity. Next came the rain pounding down in torrents. Lightning cracked from side to side - a massive overwhelming storm. In the distance I could make out a figure. It was the figure of a man and I could see he was a dancing figure. He was dancing on the waves. As he drew nearer I saw he was an Israeli. He was young. He was handsome. He had olive skin and black curly hair. His head was thrown heavenwards, his arms raised aloft. He was dancing on the waves, a leaping, exultant, magnificent Israeli dance. He was vibrant, muscular - an Alpha male. I watched in awe as he leapt astride the waves.

He spoke:

"Do you think there is any situation I have not triumphed over?"

"I have triumphed over rape. I have triumphed over violent death. I have triumphed over everything."

"I was with them in that carnage just as I was with My servant Stephen as they pounded his body with the rocks. I was there. 'In all their affliction I was afflicted and the Angel of My Presence was with them.'"[1&2]

There is grace for everything, even violent death.

I looked again. I saw another figure in the sea. Only her hair was visible, it streamed out across the waves. She was drowning. The Lord Jesus reached down and gently pulled her up. ***"I am the Lord over everything,"*** He said. ***"Come and dance with Me."***

I was engulfed in an awesome calm. It covered me like a blanket. I rose up, dried my eyes and began to worship.

It has been quite hard for me to write about this even though nearly forty years have passed. It is not an experience I talk about often. I still do not fully understand it. All I know is that at that moment the fear of death, even violent death, left me. Once again I was able to submit to a Holy God and say with Job: ***"The Lord has given, the Lord has taken away. Blessed be the Name of the Lord. Shall we accept good at the hand of the Lord and not accept adversity?" "In all this Job did not sin, neither did he blame God."***[3]

What a man? His response to physical torment, grief and loss was to worship God.

The vision of Jesus I saw really comforted me. His appearance was quite unlike anything I had seen portrayed in art. Typically he was shown with fair hair and blue eyes. He usually wore a nebulous white gown and looked sorrowful. This portrayal always angered me. The Jesus of the art galleries looked feeble and ineffectual. To then see this vibrant, triumphant, charismatic Jesus rejoiced my heart then as it rejoices my heart today. Yes! Give it up for the Jewishness of Jesus!

"My beloved is white and ruddy
Chief among ten thousand.
His head is like the finest gold;
His locks are wavy
And black as a raven.

His eyes are like doves
By the rivers of waters,
Washed with milk, and fitly set.
His cheeks are like a bed of spices,
Banks of scented herbs... ...
His countenance is like Lebanon,
Excellent as the cedars."

(Song of Songs 5:10-13, 15)

Of course, He is not like that now. Our Saviour is unbelievably awesome. His eyes flame like fire and from His mouth a sharp two-edged sword. On His head are many kingly crowns. He is all conquering, all powerful, the only wise God, the Ruler of the universe. Rightly do we give Him all reverence and homage?

1. The martyrdom of Stephen Acts Chapter 8

2. *"In all their affliction He was afflicted, and the Angel of His Presence saved them. In His love and His pity He redeemed them: He bore and carried them..."* **(Isaiah 63:9).**

3. Job 1:21 On the death of his children and the loss of all his property.

Chapter 11

THE BLOOD OF THE MARTYRS IS THE SEED OF THE CHURCH

One family survived the massacre. They lived because they were back in the United Kingdom on deputation and training. The leaders of the Elim Mission in Katerere 1977 were Peter and Brenda Griffiths, they were both teachers. And at the time of the slaughter Peter was studying for his MA. They had two young sons, Philip and Stephen on whom the massacre had a severe and lasting impact. Thirty eight years on Stephen, now himself a medical missionary decided to seek out the facts and find out exactly what happened and who was responsible. His account in the book 'The Axe and the Tree', was published in 2017 exactly forty years after this ferocious attack.

Immediately after the tragedy, Peter Griffths had flown back to the mission station to bury the dead and sort out their affairs. At the funeral as 13 battered bodies were laid to rest Peter Griffiths offered forgiveness to the killers. He said, "We long that those who did this will come to know and love the

Lord and share heaven with those they killed, as the Apostle Paul shares heaven with the first martyr, Stephen." Some years later he was to meet some of their murderers and hear that his longings had been met. It was when he met their leader that he heard about the prayers and forgiveness that his dying victims had uttered. In the words of Stephen Griffiths, "As the cruel work of the executioners began to make ever more savage inroads on their bodies, as they endured despoliation and battering, they cried to God continually to forgive and save those who were hurting them so dreadfully"

I read that fifteen young men were the killers. What breaks ones heart is to discover that the leader was just eighteen years old, the son of a Christian pastor and a public school boy named Garikai. He called himself Devil Hondo (War Devil.) He had run away from school to join the ZANLA (Zimbabwe African National Liberation Army) guerillas in Mozambique. There together with hundreds of young idealists fighting for their country, he embarked on a life of savagery, drugs and immorality and demon worship. By his own admission, "We were possessed by demons." Of the gang of fifteen, two were killed shortly after the massacre in guerilla warfare. A further two died of drug and alcohol overdose. The remaining nine stayed in close contact, as Rhodesia became Zimbabwe under Robert Mugabe and "white" rule ended.

These young men were riddled with guilt and remorse. They could find no peace. At twenty two, Devil Hondo was "drinking, doing drugs and going with whores" (His words). But like each of his friends, he could not rid himself of the cries of the children they had beaten to death, and the prayers of forgiveness uttered by the missionaries even as they screamed in pain.

One evening as the nine met together in a common bond of guilt and misery, suddenly and simultaneously, each of them saw a vision of the cross of the Lord Jesus Christ. Devil Hondo screamed out in terror fearing the judgment of God. Together with the others, he cried out for mercy and as he did so, the peace of God descended and he experienced for himself the love and mercy of our forgiving God.

Devil Hondo renounced his life of crime and hatred. He took back his birth name Garikai. Some years later, he sought the forgiveness and friendship of Peter Griffiths who had reestablished the school and brought it to new and higher levels. Garikai and several of the gang went to Bible School and became preachers of the love of God. Until he died in 1993, Peter Griffiths mentored and guided Garikai in his Christian walk.

The last member of the group to succumb to the claims of Christ was Chenjerai Mupedzisi. Three years after the massacre, he was severely injured in a road accident, which rendered him paraplegic. He became violent and aggressive but inside he was longing for peace. One night he disturbed everyone in the hospital with his screams for mercy. A hospital worker was able to minister God's love and forgiveness to him. He now shares his story of God's redeeming love all over Zimbabwe.

I will close this chapter with words from Dr. Stephen Griffiths:

"Our pain is real pain, and our loss is grievous and life-long. But in the hands of God, the suffering of His children endured on the path of faithful obedience can bring about unexpected, unlooked for results. The death of a seed, planted in sorrow, and watered with tears, can produce a harvest of righteousness, joy, and gratitude to God."

Chapter 12
DISCIPLINE

***"My son, do not regard lightly the discipline of the Lord. Nor faint when you are reproved by Him. For those who the Lord loves He disciplines and scourges every son whom He receive. It is for discipline that you endure; God deals with you as sons: For what son is there whom his father does not discipline?"* (Hebrews 12:5-7 ASV).**

At the time, discipline can seem very irksome but God loves us enough to persist.

His standards are VERY high; His ways higher than our ways. His standard is,

"Be ye perfect as your Father in heaven is perfect."

I am not qualified to comment on that, but I feel what I want to share would not be complete without some form of follow up and it's mostly about discipline.

Firstly on the question, "Are you willing to surrender EVERYTHING to God?"

As I have said I had an extremely happy carefree childhood but I was rarely disciplined. I mostly did as I pleased. God had to put some backbone into me and that is why He wanted me to go through the rigours of the 1950s' nursing regime. If nothing else, I learned about sheer hard work and commitment.

Interestingly after the "born again' experience, I began to enjoy nursing, so much so that I went on to become a qualified a midwife.

Secondly "Are you willing to be single and celibate?"

After my encounter with the Holy Spirit at the Bible College when He asked me to be willing to be single I was quite euphoric. I was on a high. I felt so pleased with myself. I had given away XYZ and now the 'supreme sacrifice,' singleness and celibacy. It's laughable now but I felt I must be one of God's favourites! I remember a conversation:

"Lord, I have given away all my money, and everything valuable, now I'm not even going to marry. You must be so pleased with me. I'm still a virgin and I will be a virgin all my life." (It was only His grace) Then I went into overdrive: "I could never be a prostitute, so disgusting. I don't know how they could live like that."

Imagine my horror when the Holy Spirit retorted:

"There is something worse than prostitution, and you are full of it. It's called pride. I resist the proud but I give grace to the humble."

My eyes were opened. I was undone. I had to agree I was indeed brimful of pride and arrogance.

A little while later I prayed a dangerous prayer. "Lord show me my heart." He showed me. It was a can of worms. I saw myself in all my wickedness and cried out for mercy. When God says: ***"The heart is deceitful and DESPERATELY wicked. Who can know it?"*** He knows what He is talking about.

After that, I actually felt like the Apostle Paul - the chief of sinners. Having seen the true nature of my unrepentant self, I felt even more grateful to a Holy God who deigned to lavish His love upon me,

"Those who have been forgiven much, love much."

Regarding marriage, after all the turmoil of our courtship and the struggle to marry, I had imagined that hand in hand to the background of sweet music we would somehow float away into a state of unending bliss. Well, dear reader, it was not like that! No question that we loved each other. No question that it was God who was our matchmaker, but in the early days and in the midst of many amazing things outside, at home it was "fight the good fight with all your might."

Again, I admit I was offended with God.

But commitment, stickability and desperation are great things. So is the grace of God. Eventually we came to a glorious place of harmony. ***"If two of you harmonise on earth about anything it shall be given you."***

It is then that we found His yoke is easy and His burden is light,

Looking at Part 3 "Are you willing to go back to Nigeria?"

It did not work out at all the way I had expected. We were only there for one more year before we found ourselves back in England. It was without doubt the most difficult year of our lives. Our two children nearly died. They were desperately ill. In fact, we think Simon left us but as we shouted and shouted to God, his spirit miraculously returned. We had very little money. Our living conditions were primitive. Yet through it all, I was still on a high. Yet within a year, we were back. Yet again I was offended with God.

Why were we back? It was God's discipline. He had more lessons for both us to learn. For me it was my old enemy, arrogance; this time spiritual arrogance. I became guilty of spiritual superiority.

Thank God for His discipline. He told me in no uncertain terms that I just was not cutting it either as a wife or a mother. He reminded me that my first calling was not to be Katherine Kuhlman but to be firstly a wife, and then a mother. He told me to step aside from the ministry for two years and concentrate on my role as wife and mother. Attitudes are important to God. I really thank Him for His correction. Yes, for His discipline.

After two years of correction and conviction we were both in a much better place. It was then that we returned for a third time to Nigeria. This time it was an entirely different story. Harmony is a wonderful thing. I guess by now we had learned that is it only by the Holy Spirit we live and move and have our being and that without Him we can do nothing.

Finally what was the outcome of my encounter with the Victorious Lord?

Thankfully the gang rape in Ibadan at the time stopped as quickly as it started. My husband returned and our work building (literally!) a branch of the Four Square Gospel Church prospered. It is still going well today.

I have never suffered any violence but the experience impacted me deeply. I now realize that there is no such thing as "easy believism."

The Christian life is no sinecure. When we sign up we are expected to live like the Lord Jesus Christ; to enter into ***"the fellowship of His sufferings."***

I love the hymn written by George Matheson in 1882 He graduated from Glasgow University with first class honours. He was in love and engaged to be married. He was worried that his sight was failing. On visiting the optician he was told that very soon he would be totally blind. When his fiancé heard the news she broke off the engagement saying. "I do not want to be the wife of a blind man." Utterly broken and in anguish this is what he wrote:

O Love that will not let me go,
I rest my weary soul on Thee:
I give Thee back the life I owe
That in its ocean depths it's flow
May richer fuller be.

O Joy that seekest me through pain
I cannot close my heart to Thee;
I trace the rainbow through the rain,
And feel its promise is not vain,
That morn shall tearless be.

O cross that liftest up my head
I dare not ask to fly from Thee
I lay in dust life's glory dead
And from the ground there blossoms red
Life that shall endless be.

George Matheson never married. He became a famous preacher, beloved by all including Queen Victoria.

We should be able to say with the Apostle Paul "to me to live is Christ; to die is gain," and "I am crucified with Christ nevertheless I live. And the life that I now live, I live by faith in the Son of God who loved me and died for me."

Let's remind ourselves of Charles Thomas Studd, a wealthy Cambridge graduate who played cricket for England and had a glittering life before him. He said, "If Jesus Christ be God and died for me, no sacrifice can be too great to give to Him."

As he sailed for China in 1885 he said, "Some want to live within the sound of chapel bell; I want to run a rescue shop within a yard of hell."

In his poem "only one life" he states,

"Only one life "twill soon be past.
Only what's done for Jesus will last."

EPILOGUE

A small child toddles to her father. He runs to meet her arm outstretched, throws her up in the air and twirls her round and round.

Over fifty years later grandma is putting her first grandchild to bed. Her name is Zoe. She is just two years old. They are the only ones in the house; everyone else has travelled. Grandma is relishing every moment. Zoe splashes in the bath; both of them jump on the bed. It's time to sleep. Zoe lies in her cot, grandma sings to her. Grandma reads her stories. Grandma prays with her. Grandma is having fun.

The fun comes to sudden end.

"Grandma I'm really tired. Can I go to sleep now?"

And with that Zoe firmly shuts her eyes and sleeps.

Grandma is dumbfounded. In all her years of raising boys, she never had such a request. Disappointed, she kneels by the cot and gazes at the sleeping child.

Grandma says,

"Father I'm overwhelmed with love for this little granddaughter. I can almost feel my heart jumping out of my chest."

"What kind of love is it?"

"It's such a passionate love. The depth of feeling is surprising."

"What else?"

"Well, it's an admiring love. She is so perfect. I'm looking at the eyelashes on the little fat cheeks. I'm looking at the tiny finger nails and the intricate convolutions of the ears."

"And?"

"It's a protective love. I'm the only one here who can defend her if there is an intruder. I need to sleep with one ear open in case she is ill in the night."

"Kate, when your head hits the pillow I do what you are doing.

All night long I watch over you with a passionate love. To Me you are My child. I gaze on you with admiration for I formed and chose you. I never slumber. I never sleep. All night long I sing over you, rejoice over you, watch over you. And in the morning I hope that your first words will be 'Daddy, Daddy.'"

These words are echoed in Zephaniah 3:17

"The Lord your God in the midst, the Mighty One will save; He will rejoice over you with gladness, He will quiet you with His love, He will rejoice over you with singing."

DOXOLOGY

"Now unto Him who is able to keep you from falling and to present you faultless in the Presence of His glory with exceeding joy. To the only wise God our Saviour, be glory and majesty, dominion and power both now and forever, Amen" **(Jude 24).**

36967173R00055

Printed in Great Britain
by Amazon